PIERRE-AUGUSTE
Renoir

Paintings

LEOPARD

This edition published in 1995 by Leopard Books
Random House, 20 Vauxhall Bridge Road, London SW1V 2SA

ISBN 0 7529 0035 8
Printed and bound in Portugal by
Printer Portuguesa Lda

"Believe me: it is possible to paint everything. To be sure, it is better to paint a pretty girl or a pleasing landscape. But anything can be a subject." [1]

—PIERRE-AUGUSTE RENOIR

1. *After Lunch* 1879

2. *Lise with a Parasol* 1867

3. *Portrait of Mlle. Irène Cahen D'Anvers* 1880

4. *Looking out at Sacre-Coeur* 1896

5. *A Large Vase of Flowers*

6. *Landscape in Algiers* 1881

7. *Mediterranean Fruits* 1881

8. *Portrait of Actress Jeanne Samary* 1878

9. *Portrait of Margot* c. 1878

10. *Road Climbing Through High Grass* 1875

11. *Moulin Huet Bay, Guernsey*

12. *Girl with a Hoop* 1885

13. *The Umbrellas* 1881-85

14. *Girl in a Boat*

15. *Claude Monet Reading*

16. *Young Girls at The Piano* 1892

17. *Vase of Roses*

18. *Madame Charpentier and her Children* 1878

19. *Dance in the Country* 1885

20. *Dance in the City* 1883

21. *The Seine at Asnieres*

22. *At "La Grenouilliere"* 1879

23. *The Bouquet*

24. *A Bouquet of Flowers*

25. *Gabriella with a Rose*

26. *Gabrielle with Jean* 1900

27. *Nude in a Chair*

28. *Two Bathers*

29. *Bathers*

30. *Woman with a Cat*

31. *The Lerolle Sisters*

Afterword

Pierre-Auguste Renoir, born in Limoges in 1841, grew up in the shadow of the Louvre and the Tuileries when his family moved to Paris in search of a better life. The son of a poor tailor, Renoir got a job as a painter of fine porcelain at the age of ten. As a young man, often on the brink of poverty, Renoir applied the skills he acquired in this job to other decorative work, embellishing fans, curtains, and moveable altars. The light brushstrokes, the delicate pinks, brilliant blues, and chrome yellow used in porcelain, and the pastoral scenes he reproduced on vases and plates, copied from the works of Watteau, Boucher, and other masters of the rococo, had an enduring effect on Renoir's artistic achievements. Renoir became a magician of light and color. In his paintings, "The light takes on material qualities, it foams and sparkles in his pictures, and sometimes illuminates the colors like precious stones."[2]

At twenty-one Renoir registered for courses at the Ecole de Beaux-Arts and joined other young artists—including Bazille, Sisley, and Monet—at the Gleyre Studio. Monet and Renoir quickly became known as revolutionaries among the students, as they overturned the canons of traditional art by rejecting its demands for "dignified" subject matter, balanced composition, precise drawing, and somber coloration. Following the lead of Courbet and Manet, they depicted the contemporary scene and, seeking to capture the transient quality of nature in a realistic manner, they set up their easels in the Fontainebleau Woods near Chailly, transferring what they perceived directly to their canvases. Throughout the 1860s, Renoir's paintings were accepted by the official Salon of Paris. *Lise with a Parasol* (plate 2) was shown at the 1868 Salon; remarkable in its technical excellence, it broke new ground in both its subject matter and coloring. As the critic Thore-Buerger wrote, "The effect is so natural and true that one might very well find it false, because one is accustomed to nature represented in conventional colors." [3]

As students, Renoir and Monet shared quarters in Paris, and Renoir frequently joined Monet in Argenteuil during the 1870s. One of the few Renoir canvases that remains from the early 1870s is his *Claude Monet Reading* (plate 15). Despite later artistic differences, the two remained life-long friends. Together, Renoir and Monet translated the light and color they saw into works of art. The dark, heavy colors he had adopted from Courbet lightened and the contours of objects blurred as Renoir concentrated on recreating the play of light and shadows.

Renoir was not an intellectual artist; he believed in experiment, not theory. He painted for pleasure—to please himself *and* spectators, perhaps a legacy of his work as decorative artist where pleasing the customer was of the utmost importance. But though he was bored by their theoretical discussions about art,[4] like Pissarro, Cézanne, Monet, Manet, and Degas, Renoir was dedicated to the tenets of the Independent movement. When his submissions were rejected by the Salon in 1872 and 1873, Renoir became one of the leaders in organizing the first show of the Independents: the notorious 1874 Exhibition that gave birth to the term

"Impressionist." Seven of his paintings were shown there; fifteen were included in the second Impressionist Exhibition held in 1876. One of these, *The Dance at the Moulin de la Gallette* (back cover), conveys an element of Renoir's sensibilities matched by no other painter of the period—his fascination with people, whom he endowed with genuine warmth and *joie de vivre*.

Discouraged by the public antipathy and critical censure that greeted the Impressionist exhibitions, and motivated in part by a pressing need to earn money, Renoir turned to the less controversial and more profitable work of portraiture. He received many commissions from the art dealer Durand-Ruel as well as patrons of the arts like Cailleboite, Choquet, and Charpentier. He was particularly in demand for portraits of children: *Portrait of Mlle. Irène Cahen d'Anvers* (plate 3) is one of the finest examples of Renoir's ability to re-create the delicate beauty of young girls. At the official Salon of 1879, *Madame Charpentier and her Children* (plate 18) caught the attention of the novelist Marcel Proust who admired its "somber opulence."[5] While Renoir clearly sought to achieve an accurate physical resemblance in this portrait, its informal liveliness—as though the painter had caught the subjects between movements—marks a new sophistication in the history of portraiture.

The next decade (called the "dry period" by art historians) was a time of experimentation for Renoir. He later wrote, "I had followed Impressionism to the utmost limits and was forced to come to the conclusion that I could neither paint nor draw. I had reached a dead end."[6] He traveled to North Africa and while the paintings he created there—for example, *Landscape in Algiers* (plate 6)—retain certain Impressionist brush techniques, they are more carefully structured and more densely worked than his paintings of the previous decade. Inspired by the Raphael frescos he saw on a trip to Italy in 1881, Renoir began to work in a larger format and took renewed interest in the clarity of composition and the beauty of the line. *The Umbrellas* (plate 13), painted between 1881-5, shows Renoir in transition; while the figures on the right are strictly Impressionist in style, in those on the left Renoir emphasized the contrasts of rounded surfaces and the rigid edges of the objects. In *Dance in the City* (plate 20), executed in 1883, forms are clearly distinguished and the colors lack the vibrancy of Renoir's "pure" Impressionist paintings.

Hoping to create the "simplicity and grandeur" of Raphael's frescos, Renoir turned to the timeless themes of women and children. His future wife, a perfect example of the plump, rounded Renoir woman, served as a model for such paintings as *Dance in the Country* (plate 19). *The Bathers* (plate 29) represents the stylistic and artistic climax of this period. As Bruno F. Schneider writes, "The wonderful harmony of movement of the figures...is reminiscent of Classicist relief, and the many intersections of the legs of the two sitting girls are so balanced that they give the impression of belonging...to a choreographic study."[7] Renoir had returned to the studio to work, having come to believe, "An artist who paints straight from nature is really looking for nothing but momentary effects. He does not try to be creative and, as a result, the pictures soon become monotonous."[8]

This return to traditional painting techniques and the transition from the dominance of color to the dominance of line revitalized

Renoir's works. By the end of the 1880s, however, Renoir faced a more profound crisis. Attempting to reintroduce color while retaining his mastery of form, he often produced paintings that lacked the spontaneity and grace for which he is so admired. Slowly and painfully, Renoir emerged from this difficult period. In paintings like *Young Girls at the Piano* (plate 16) and portraits of his own children like *Gabrielle with Jean* (plate 26), his technique became softer and more painterly. Writing about the latter work, Renoir said, "One must be personally involved with what one does.... At the moment I am painting Jean pouting. It's no easy thing but it's a lovely subject." [9] Still-lifes of flowers and fruits provided Renoir with a respite from the demands of painting the human figure. "When I paint flowers," he told his friend Georges Riviere, "my mind has a rest.... I put different shades of color and try out some bold tonal values, without worrying about spoiling a canvas." [10]

Renoir's artistic crisis was ironically accompanied by public triumph. Successful exhibitions were held at the Durand-Ruel gallery in 1892 and in 1896, and in 1900, Renoir was made a *chevalier de la legion d'honneur*. International acclaim soon followed: 59 of his paintings were exhibited in London in 1905 and in 1907 the Metropolitan Museum of Art purchased *Madame Charpentier and her Children* for a vast sum of money. [11]

Even the rheumatism that crippled his hands at the turn of the century did not prevent Renoir from painting. His late works are almost classical in their beauty: quiet, simple, they glow with a richness that epitomizes Renoir's particular genius. On his small estate in Cagnes, Renoir turned his attention once again to the beauty of the nude female body. He told his son, Jean, "What I like is skin, a young girl's skin that is pink and shows she has good circulation. But what I like above all is serenity."[12] He continued to use a model, but "he scarcely looked at her; the visions appeared before his inner eye, and found their way onto the canvas."[13] Limiting himself to only a few colors, Renoir produced luminous portraits of women as he saw them in life: blooming, alive with the joy and the tasks of living, animated by a natural beauty as real and as eternal as nature itself.

Renoir's joy in painting remained to the end of his life; he was working on a painting of flowers when he died at Cagnes on December 3, 1919.

NOTES

1. Renoir's last words, quoted by Jean Renoir, *Renoir, My Father* (San Francisco: Mercury House, Inc.), 117
2. Bruno F. Schneider, *Renoir* (New York: Crown Publishers, Inc.), 6
3. Patrick Bade, *Renoir: The Masterworks* (New York: Portland House), 52
4. Schneider, p. 22
5. Jan Rewald, *The History of Impressionism* (New York: The Museum of Modern Art), 419
6. Schneider, 68
7. Ibid, 82
8. Bade, 26
9. Ibid, 126
10. Ibid, 34
11. Ibid, 36
12. Renoir, 104
13. Schneider, 88

List of Plates

The photographs in this book were supplied by: